W9-BZI-728

Understanding

The Outsiders

New and future titles in the Understanding Great Literature series include:

Understanding

The Outsiders

UNDERSTANDING GREAT LITERATURE

Todd Howard

Lucent Books
P.O. Box 289011
San Diego, CA 92198-9011

On cover: S. E. Hinton, author of *The Outsiders.*

Library of Congress Cataloging-in-Publication Data

Howard, Todd, 1964–
  The outsiders / by Todd Howard.
    p. cm. — (Understanding great literature)
  Includes bibliographical references and index.
  Summary: Discusses the novel, "The Outsiders," including the life
of its author, S. E. Hinton, and the novel's historical background,
plot, characters, themes, and literary analysis.
  ISBN 1-56006-702-0
  1. Hinton, S. E. Outsiders—Juvenile literature. 2. Alienation
(Social psychology) in literature—Juvenile literature. 3. Brothers
in literature—Juvenile literature. 4. Orphans in literature—
Juvenile literature. 5. Boys in literature—Juvenile literature. [1.
Hinton, S. E. Outsiders. 2. American literature—History and criticism.] I. Title. II. Series.
  PS3558.I548 O986 2001
  813'.54—dc21

00-009238

Copyright 2001 by Lucent Books, Inc.
P.O. Box 289011, San Diego, California 92198-9011

Printed in the U.S.A.

Contents

FOREWORD

"Except for a living man, there is nothing more wonderful than a book!" wrote the widely respected nineteenth-century teacher and writer Charles Kingsley. A book, he continued, "is a message to us from human souls we never saw. And yet these [books] arouse us, terrify us, teach us, comfort us, open our hearts to us as brothers." There are many different kinds of books, of course; and Kingsley was referring mainly to those containing literature—novels, plays, short stories, poems, and so on. In particular, he had in mind those works of literature that were and remain widely popular with readers of all ages and from many walks of life.

Such popularity might be based on one or several factors. On the one hand, a book might be read and studied by people in generation after generation because it is a literary classic, with characters and themes of universal relevance and appeal. Homer's epic poems, the *Iliad* and the *Odyssey*, Chaucer's *Canterbury Tales*, Shakespeare's *Hamlet* and *Romeo and Juliet*, and Dickens's *A Christmas Carol* fall into this category. Some popular books, on the other hand, are more controversial. Mark Twain's *Huckleberry Finn* and J. D. Salinger's *The Catcher in the Rye*, for instance, have their legions of devoted fans who see them as great literature; while others view them as less than worthy because of their racial depictions, profanity, or other factors.

Still another category of popular literature includes realistic modern fiction, including novels such as Robert Cormier's *I Am the Cheese* and S. E. Hinton's *The Outsiders*. Their keen social insights and sharp character portrayals have consistently reached out to and captured the imaginations of many teenagers and young adults; and for this reason they are often assigned and studied in schools.

These and other similar works have become the "old standards" of the literary scene. They are the ones that people most often read, discuss, and study; and each has, by virtue of its content, critical success, or just plain longevity, earned the right to be the subject of a book examining its content. (Some, of course, like the *Iliad* and *Hamlet*, have been the subjects of numerous books already; but their literary stature is so lofty that there can never be too many books about them!) For millions of readers and students in one generation after another, each of these works becomes, in a sense, an adventure in appreciation, enjoyment, and learning.

The main purpose of Lucent's Understanding Great Literature series is to aid the reader in that ongoing literary adventure. Each volume in the series focuses on a single literary work that a majority of critics and teachers view as a classic and/or that is widely studied and discussed in schools. A typical volume first tells why the work in question is important. Then follow detailed overviews of the author's life, the work's historical background, its plot, its characters, and its themes. Numerous quotes from the work, as well as by critics and other experts, are interspersed throughout and carefully documented with footnotes for those who wish to pursue further research. Also included is a list of ideas for essays and other student projects relating to the work, an appendix of literary criticisms and analyses by noted scholars, and a comprehensive annotated bibliography.

The great nineteenth-century American poet Henry David Thoreau once quipped: "Read the best books first, or you may not have a chance to read them at all." For those who are reading or about to read the "best books" in the literary canon, the comprehensive, thorough, and thoughtful volumes of the Understanding Great Literature series are indispensable guides and sources of enrichment.

Inside *The Outsiders*

W hen S. E. Hinton's novel about an orphaned, underprivileged teenager's search for identity amid violent gang life was published in 1967, it marked a significant departure indeed from the status quo of young adult literature. While innocent topics such as raising horses and even potentially perilous subjects such as drag racing and dating had all been considered at length in young adult novels by the mid-1960s, the publishing industry's assumptions about the interests and maturity level of teen readers had never allowed for the degree of sobering realism found in *The Outsiders*.

Thus, the overwhelming commercial success that *The Outsiders* enjoyed among teens shortly after its first publication sent astounded publishers scurrying to find writers who could duplicate the novel's formula, and gave pause to literary critics. The novel's commercial success quickly opened a Pandora's box of mature themes in young adult literature, and the resulting genre, alternately referred to as "Problem Books" and "the New Realism," has since produced countless titles. And although switchblade-toting, cigarette-smoking rebels in *The Outsiders* may seem somewhat tame in comparison with the teen characters in some of these subsequent contributions to the genre, the novel's appeal to teen readers has remained wide ranging and vital—so much so, in fact, it remains the best-selling young adult novel of all time and has been adapted into both a prime-time television series and a commercially successful motion picture.

While the novel's plot recalls the animosity that existed between underprivileged "greasers" and affluent "Socs" in Hinton's hometown of Tulsa during the mid-1960s, it also speaks to the socioeconomic divisions that have continued in American society to the present day. (And if the fact that the story has been translated into a half-dozen languages is any indication, one can assume that it also speaks to such divisions elsewhere.) Hinton notes of the enduring appeal of *The Outsiders,* "I was fortunate to hit on a universal theme . . . which is one of the reasons why the book is still being read today. The labels may change, but the groups go on."[1] Indeed, as they struggle for survival on the fringes of society,

Like the novel, the 1982 film The Outsiders *explored the conflict between upper class kids, or "Socs," and the less privileged "greasers," pictured here.*

the intelligent, sensitive, and idealistic Ponyboy and his fellow gang members still come as a revelation to teen readers across the socioeconomic spectrum.

As *The Outsiders* maintains its decades-old status as the archetype of realistic young adult literature, it still comes as a revelation to the literary community as well. The novel continues to receive honors from distinguished literary and educational organizations for its contributions to young adult literature, and it is also still invoked by those on both sides of the ongoing debate over censorship in young adult literature.

Though the novel once found its home far off the beaten track, *The Outsiders* has long since taken up residency in the mainstream of young adult literature. If the last three decades are any indication, the novel shall remain a prominent resident there, earning new accolades and revealing for new generations of young readers problems that are common to the teen experience on both sides of the economic divide.

CHAPTER ONE

The Life of S. E. Hinton

Susan Eloise Hinton was born on July 22, 1948, in Tulsa, Oklahoma. Her greatest loves as a child—aside from horses—were reading and writing. Hinton, who was a shy, sensitive little girl, found refuge in literature and realized early on that she wanted to be a writer when she grew up.

Hinton entered Will Rogers High School in Tulsa in 1963. As with many American towns during the early 1960s, Tulsa was sharply divided along social and economic lines, and this division was painfully evident in the animosity that existed between the underprivileged "greasers" (a gang so named for their long, greased hair) and the affluent, socially prominent "Socs" (short for "Socials") at Will Rogers High. Having always felt like something of an outsider herself due to her shyness, Hinton's sympathies tended toward her school's greasers, who were largely shunned because of their low socioeconomic standing.

Being neither a greaser or a Soc, however, Hinton found the entire social hierarchy embraced by her fellow students disturbing. She later noted, "It drove me nuts that people would get ulcers over who to say hi to in the hall."[2] Hinton had known students—both Socs and greasers—who had suffered beatings by the rival group and later noted that while she was in high school, "a real boy like [her character] Dallas Winston was shot and killed by police."[3]

Origins of *The Outsiders*

In light of her exposure to such serious social issues, as well as her sensitivity and passion for reading and writing, it comes as no surprise that Hinton found little satisfaction from the superficial young adult novels that were available to teenagers at that time. During her junior year in high school, Hinton began to write a novel about the animosity between Socs and greasers, in an effort to create the sort of young adult novel that she would enjoy reading. Ironically, that same year she received a D in her creative writing class.

It was also during this year that Hinton's world was turned upside down by her father's diagnosis of brain cancer. As her father's condition worsened, Hinton became increasingly withdrawn and began to spend more and more time immersed in writing what would become *The Outsiders*. According to Hinton's mother, "The sicker he became, the harder she worked."[4] Hinton's father died of cancer in 1965 when she was a senior in high school—little more than a year after he was diagnosed. Hinton completed *The Outsiders* during her senior year, then shelved the book as she prepared for college life.

Hinton was accepted at the University of Tulsa, where she began working toward a degree in journalism in the fall of 1966. Early in her first year at the university, she showed the completed manuscript for *The Outsiders* to a fellow student whose mother was an author. The woman liked it and gave it to a fellow writer who had an agent (at that point in time, Hinton later noted, she didn't know that literary agents existed). The agent liked it and sold it to Viking Press—the second publisher who read it.

Viking Press published *The Outsiders* the following April. Instead of using Hinton's first name, however, Viking used Hinton's first and middle initials in order to keep her gender a secret from potential male readers who—company marketers believed—were not likely to read the work of a female writer.

Susan Hinton began writing her controversial novel The Outsiders *while she was still in high school.*

The book, however, was not initially marketed toward teens, but rather adults. It wasn't until the book was discovered by teens and gained widespread popularity among them that it began to attain commercial success and critical acclaim.

Hinton's Alter Ego

Because they found the depiction of Ponyboy—the book's main character—so realistic, many readers and literary critics initially assumed that S. E. Hinton, too, was a male. Further, a sort of folklore began to emerge about her: some reviewers suggested that S. E. Hinton was in fact a greaser and that *The Outsiders* was autobiographical; others suspected that Hinton

13

had achieved the realism of *The Outsiders* through danger-ous investigative journalism. Hinton began to receive letters from her teen readers, many of which were addressed to "Ponyboy."

Though this public persona bore little resemblance to the real Hinton, she was not in a hurry to set the record straight. She instead tried to use it to protect her privacy and anonymity. Some of the myths and misconceptions about Hinton have continued to recycle among young readers throughout the years and have been bolstered by the fact that the three books that followed *The Outsiders* were also told from the point of view of tough male teens. Hinton says today, "I don't mind having two identities; in fact, I like keeping the writer part separate in some ways. And since my alter ego is clearly a 15-year-old boy, having an authorial self that doesn't suggest a gender is just fine with me."[5]

Additionally, *The Outsiders* had begun to earn Hinton a reputation as a sort of teenage wonder within the literary community. It was chosen as an honor book at the *Chicago Tribune*'s Children's Spring Book Festival and was also select-ed for the *New York Herald Tribune*'s Best Teenage Books list. Though it was difficult for her due to her shyness, she began to make appearances at book conventions and to give media interviews.

Hinton's celebrity status was furthered by her essay "Teenagers Are for Real." In this essay, which appeared in the *New York Times Book Review* in August 1967, four months after the first publication of *The Outsiders*, Hinton argues that teenagers crave, and are entitled to, realistic fiction. She accus-es the young adult genre of having fallen many years behind the times, presenting subject matter that grossly underesti-mates the maturity level of teens.

Due to the serious subject matter and violence addressed in *The Outsiders* and the strong views expressed in "Teenagers Are for Real," Hinton found that her name and work were becoming invoked in the ongoing censorship debate between conservatives and those who, as with Hinton, felt that the status quo of young adult literature was condescending to teens. Literary critic John S. Simmons notes of *The Outsiders:* "To the smug, would-be book banners of the times . . . , its most objectionable trait is the constant reliance on violence to deal with problems."[6] But Hinton felt that young readers were sophisticated enough to perceive the book's underlying sentiment that violence is destructive and self-defeating.

Life After *The Outsiders*

In 1968 Hinton published a short story entitled "Rumble Fish," which is about a teenager named Rusty-James who has a rugged motorcycle-riding older brother who was always there to get him out of trouble. Hinton had been inspired to write the story by a photo that she had seen in a magazine of a rough-looking young man on a motorcycle. Aside from this short story, however, she did little creative writing for several years after *The Outsiders*. The success of the novel and the celebrity status and controversy it had generated for her left her feeling pressured and suffering from writer's block. Consequently, she had decided to dedicate all of her energy to her college studies.

At some point in her academic career, Hinton changed her college major from journalism to education and began studies to become a teacher. While pursuing this goal, however, she had doubts concerning her suitability as an educator. "I don't have the nerve or physical stamina to teach," she would later note. "I did my student teaching, but I couldn't leave the kids and their problems behind me; I'd go home and worry about them."[7]

While in college, Hinton met her future husband, David Inhofe, whom she would later credit with curing her writer's block and keeping alive her desire to write. While they were dating, Inhofe would refuse to take her out unless she had written two pages that day. Thus, over the course of four months, Hinton compiled the manuscript that would become *That Was Then, This Is Now*—a full-length novel about drugs, delinquency, and kids making difficult decisions. Though Hinton felt certain that she did not want to teach, she completed her degree in education and graduated from the University of Tulsa in the spring of 1970. She married David Inhofe the following September.

Hinton Resumes Her Writing Career

That Was Then, This Is Now was published in 1971. The book became an honor book at the *Chicago Tribune*'s Children's Spring Book Festival that year and was also selected for the American Library Association's Best Books for Young Adults list. After the book's publication, Hinton and her new husband traveled in Europe for six months, after which they moved to Palo Alto, California, in order for David to complete his degree

Hinton had a small role in the movie Tex, *based on her novel of the same name. Pictured here are Hinton and actor Matt Dillon, who played Tex.*

at Stanford University. After David graduated in 1973, they moved back to Tulsa.

In 1975 Hinton expanded "Rumble Fish" into a full-length novel. It, too, received immediate accolades, including being selected for the American Library Association's and the *School Library Journal*'s Best Books of the Year lists. *The Outsiders*, for its part, was still receiving awards, such as *Media and Methods* magazine's Maxi Award.

During the next several years, Hinton worked on another novel entitled *Tex*, which deals with two teenage brothers who are forced to cope with the absence of their traveling father. When *Tex* was published in 1979, it received numerous literary awards and was also selected for the American Library Association's and *School Library Journal*'s Best Books lists.

Hollywood Discovers Hinton

The year 1982 would mark something of a turning point in Hinton's career. Her work had begun to draw the interest of the movie industry, and during the next three years, four of her novels would be made into feature films. Hinton was involved in various capacities in the making of these films, including casting, scriptwriting, directing, and even acting. Commenting on how fortunate she felt for being able to participate in the making of the film versions of her work, she told a *Los Angeles Times* reporter, "Once I sold the books I expected to be asked to drop off the face of the earth, but that didn't happen. I know that I had extremely rare experiences for a writer."[8]

In September 1982 Disney released a film version of *Tex* starring Matt Dillon. Not only did Hinton have a small acting role in the film herself, but one of Hinton's conditions for allowing Disney to adapt *Tex* into a film was that they use her horse Toyota in the filming. Hinton taught Dillon to ride horseback for his role and later said of him, "Boy that kid

Hinton insisted that her own horse be used in the film version of Tex. *She herself taught Matt Dillon (pictured with her horse, Toyota) to ride.*

caught on quick. My horse loved him. He'd knock me down to get to that kid. It was irritating."[9] Hinton and Dillon became friends during the filming of *Tex* and still maintain their friendship.

In March 1983 a film version of *The Outsiders* was released by Warner Brothers. Hinton cowrote the screenplay for the film with the film's director, Francis Ford Coppola. The movie stars Matt Dillon, Ralph Macchio, C. Thomas Howell, Patrick Swayze, Rob Lowe, Emilio Estevez, Tom Cruise, and Leif Garrett and also features a cameo appearance by Hinton. Hinton also served as a paid consultant for Coppola during the filming. The film was a commercial success, grossing $5 million during the first weekend it was released.

In August 1983 Hinton gave birth to her son, Nicholas David. The extent of Hinton's fame was illustrated by Nicholas's birth being announced in the "Milestones" column of *Time* magazine. Nick's birth, however, would mark a sharp decrease in the amount of traveling Hinton would do for public appearances and interviews.

A film version of *Rumble Fish* was released by Universal Studios in October 1983. As with *The Outsiders*, the screenplay for the film was cowritten by Hinton and Coppola and was

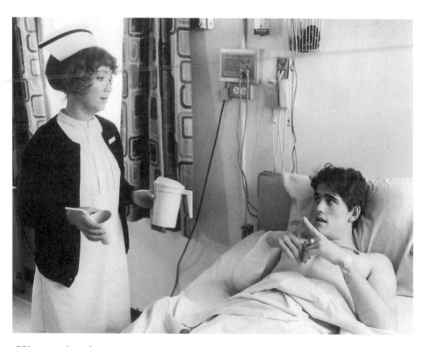

Hinton played a nurse in the film adaptation of The Outsiders.

directed by Coppola. The film stars Matt Dillon, Mickey Rourke, Dennis Hopper, Christopher Penn, and Tom Waits. This film was also a commercial success, as was the highly acclaimed musical score for the film, which was composed and performed by Stewart Copeland of the popular rock band The Police.

In November 1985 a film version of *That Was Then, This Is Now* was released by Paramount Studios. Actor Emilio Estevez wrote the screenplay for the film and costars in the film with Morgan Freeman. This same year, Fox Television aired a television series based on *The Outsiders*.

Hinton's fifth book, *Taming the Star Runner*, was published in October 1988. The book marked a stylistic departure for her, in that it was the first of her stories that wasn't told from the point of view of the main character. "My son, Nick, was then four," Hinton later said of this decision, "and I was so involved with him that I didn't have the emotional space to become a completely other person."[10] The story is about a teenager named Travis who admires the courage that a young woman shows as she tries to tame a wild horse named Star Runner.

In 1988 Hinton also received the American Library Association/*School Library Journal*'s first annual Margaret A. Edwards Award. The purpose of the award was to honor the careers of authors whose work over a period of time has been accepted by young people as an authentic voice that continues to illuminate their experiences and emotions, giving insight into their lives.

Exploring New Genres

After *Taming the Star Runner* was published, Hinton took a seven-year break from fiction writing and wrote instead in other genres. Hinton says of this era, "I couldn't think of a single thing to say. I didn't have a writer's block—I was writing plenty: screenplays for my novels, television scripts, advertisements. I simply didn't have a story I wanted to tell."[11]

Another story did eventually come to her. It was even more of a departure from her earlier works than *Taming the Star Runner* had been. Far from being a story about teenage boys on the fringes of society, it was a picture book for young children. Hinton got the idea for the book from an incident that occurred when her son, Nick, was entering kindergarten.

Actors in a 1985 Fox Television series based on The Outsiders.

21

During his first day at school, Nick met a boy who, like Nick's father, had dark hair, glasses, and was named David. Nick playfully asked his father if the little boy was, in fact, him. Playing along, Nick's father told him that he and the little boy were in fact the same person. Hinton used this episode as the premise for *Big David, Little David,* a whimsical, humorous story about confused identities and a battle of wits between a little boy and his father. Hinton collaborated on *Big David, Little David* with illustrator Alan Daniel.

In 1995 Hinton collaborated with illustrator Jacqueline Rogers on another children's story. "Nick is an only child," Hinton explains of this book's premise,

> and was not an animal person. He was a little bit afraid of dogs, but I was determined to get him a puppy so he could connect and share attention in the family. We got our puppy when Nick was eight, and there was so much sibling rivalry between the two that he once accused me of loving the dog more than I loved him. "Honey," I told him, "it's not true. I love you more: you're housebroken."[12]

Hinton knew she was on to something with this premise of puppy-boy rivalry but felt that the plot needed something more to make a successful children's story. One day Nick said to Hinton of their puppy, Alesha, "I wonder when she will turn into a person." This was the missing link in the plot that Hinton had been seeking for the story. The result was *The Puppy Sister*, Hinton's seventh book, published in 1995.

While Hinton has spent the majority of her time since then with her son, involving herself primarily with his life and education, her favorite pastimes have largely remained those that she enjoyed as a young girl: reading, writing, and horses. Hinton has continued taking university courses and has also learned to play piano. "I'm not any one thing," Hinton now says of herself, and that's a reason I don't mind having a separate identity for my writing. I'm an author, but I'm also a mother, a friend, a horseback rider, a decent cook. Being involved domestically keeps me in touch with reality.[13]

Thus, it seems that Hinton's early efforts to cope with being an outsider have ultimately led her to a life and career in which she feels very much at home.

CHAPTER TWO

Redefining Young Adult Fiction

S. E. Hinton did not begin writing *The Outsiders* with the intention of forging a new genre of young adult literature. Nor did she intend to write a book that would be part of an already heated debate regarding censorship. Furthermore, as a junior in high school during the late 1960s, Hinton could not have known that she was writing what would prove to be the best-selling young adult novel of all time, a book that would speak to the hearts of millions of teenagers for generations to come.

Rather, Hinton began to write *The Outsiders* simply because she wanted something of interest to read. She found the young adult novels that were available to her to be boring at best and wanted to read about something that mattered to her. Not surprisingly, what mattered to her was life as a teenager in her hometown of Tulsa, Oklahoma, during the mid-1960s.

The Social Underpinnings of *The Outsiders*

Among the most obvious elements of life as a teenager in Tulsa at that time was the sharp division among teens along socioeconomic lines. Hinton had seen this division reflected in her high school's two main social groups: the underprivileged "greasers," and the affluent, socially prominent "Socs." Tulsa was one of many American cities that had seen an increasing division between social classes since World War II, and the animosity between greaser and Soc gangs illustrated the extent to which this division between social classes had permeated society.

Hinton was herself neither a greaser or a Soc. Rather, she was a shy, observant girl who, from the outside looking in, could see the absurdity and destructiveness of the rivalry between these two groups. Hinton later said of her high school years:

> I didn't have any label in high school. I think I was considered a little eccentric. I'm still considered a little eccentric. If I had a label at all it was probably something like "The School Nut," but I was friends with Greasers, Socs, Artsy-Craftsies. I could talk to all of them because I wasn't any of them.[14]

Hinton biographer Jay Daly notes that Hinton had been deeply affected when a young greaser in Tulsa was shot to death by police:

> One can imagine the sixteen-year-old Susie Hinton, upset with the madness of the social sparring at her high school and the death of a boy not unlike Dallas Winston, beginning her story with much the same motivation [as Ponyboy had for writing his story].[15]

The Need for Mature Young Adult Fiction

One can also easily imagine the dissatisfaction felt by the young Hinton as she paired these serious real-life concerns with the young adult literature that was available to her. As Daly notes, the young adult literature of Hinton's time

> had for many years been dominated by books like Maureen Daly's *Seventeenth Summer,* dreamy-eyed stories of carefree youth where the major problem was

25

whether so-and-so would ask our heroine to the prom in sufficient time for her to locate a prom gown. Or there were cautionary tales to warn us that, if we were not good, and we all know what "good" meant, we would never get to the prom at all.[16]

These books and others, such as the Hardy Boys mysteries and the Nancy Drew series, had for many years provided the sort of light reading that had been widely considered as appropriate for teens such as Hinton.

Hinton, however, was not alone in her dissatisfaction with the state of young adult literature of her time. Though she didn't realize it, a heated debate had already been under way for more than a generation over the topic. Many in the literary and educational communities insisted that the superficiality in young adult literature represented a gross underestimation of the maturity level of teens, and, further, that this avoidance of serious subject matter was doing teens a disservice.

In 1965—the same year that Hinton completed *The Outsiders*—a case for more mature young adult fiction was advanced eloquently by the exalted Commission on English of the College Entrance Examination Board, as they leveled the following criticism in their widely read book *Freedom and Discipline in English:*

Claims are frequently advanced for the use of so-called "junior books," a "literature of adolescence," on the ground that they ease the young reader into a frame of mind in which he will be ready to tackle something stronger, harder, more adult. The Commission has serious doubts that it does anything of the sort. For classes in remedial reading a resort to such books may be necessary, but to make them a considerable part of the curriculum for most students is to subvert the purposes for which literature is included in the first place. In the high school years, the aim should be not to find the students' level so much as to raise it, and such books rarely elevate. For college-bound students, particularly, no such concessions as they imply are justified. Maturity of thought, vocabulary, syntax, and construction is the criterion of excellence in literature, and that criterion must not be abandoned for apparent expediency. The competent teacher can bridge the distances between good books and the immaturity of his students; that is, in fact, his primary duty as a teacher of literature.[17]

Thus, by writing *The Outsiders*, Hinton would inadvertently champion a cause that was being widely embraced by the academic and educational mainstream; her timing could not have been better.

The Birth of a Genre

While *The Outsiders* is considered to have been at the vanguard of this anticipated new era of realism in young adult fiction, its publishers did not publish it in an effort to raise the bar of realism nor did they seem to have had any inkling of the novel's commercial potential among young readers. On the contrary, Viking Press initially marketed *The Outsiders* as an adult title and with little fanfare. The overwhelming popularity that the book enjoyed among teens was exclusively the result of word of mouth. Clearly, Hinton had not been the only teen who was craving young adult fiction that portrayed the world realistically rather than formulaically, and the success of *The Outsiders* sparked a commercial interest in feeding that demand.

Due to the overwhelming popularity of *The Outsiders*, a new genre of young adult fiction, which was alternately referred to as "the New Realism" and "Problem Books," quickly arose. Hinton paved the way for best-selling titles by writers such as Paul Zindel, Richard Peck, M. E. Kerr, Paula Danziger, and Robert Cormier. However, despite the many books about such topics as divorce, abortion, and drugs and their effects on teens that began to appear en masse on library and bookstore shelves, none matched the sales and impact of *The Outsiders*.

The Censorship Debate

Notwithstanding its unprecedented sales and impact, censorship advocates weren't impressed by *The Outsiders*. They continued to insist that teens had no business reading novels containing the degree of violence and other "adult" themes featured in Hinton's book—and certainly not in the classroom. Simmons notes that such views were embraced primarily by "those parents and 'interested citizens' who demanded that only sanitized reading materials be served up to the young people in English classrooms."[18]

Hinton became even more notorious in the eyes of censorship advocates due to her essay "Teenagers Are For Real," which appeared in the August 27, 1967, edition of the *New York Times Book Review*. In it, she further champions the mature outlook of young readers and faults adults who want to ignore the realities faced by many adolescents:

> The trouble is, grownups write about teenagers from their own memories, or else write about teenagers from a stand-off, "I'm-a-little-scared-to-get-close-they're-hairy" view. The world is changing, yet the authors of books for teenagers are still 15 years behind the times.

> In the fiction they write, romance is still the most popular theme, with a-horse-and-the-girl-who-loved-it coming in a close second. Nowhere is the drive-in social jungle mentioned, the behind-the-scenes politicking that goes on in big schools, the cruel social system in which, if you can afford to snub every fourth person you meet, you're popular. In short, where is reality. . . .

> Violence too is a part of teenagers' lives. . . . Only when violence is for a sensational effect should it be

objected to in books for teenagers. Such books should not be blood and gore, but not a fairyland of proms and double-dates, either.[19]

Though Hinton couldn't have imagined in 1967 that her name would become synonymous for many with the ongoing debate over censorship in young adult literature—she didn't even realize that such a debate existed—it is in fact still invoked by parties on both sides of the debate more than thirty years after the publication of "Teenagers Are for Real" and *The Outsiders.*

Indeed, Hinton didn't begin writing *The Outsiders* with the intention of forging a new genre of young adult literature, but, without question, she has. It is neither the novel's impact on young adult literature, however, nor its involvement in the censorship debate—nor even the fact that it has sold more copies than any other young adult novel—that accounts for its ongoing popularity with teens. Rather, it is the fact that, as with the teenage Hinton of over thirty years ago, teens still find in *The Outsiders* an honest, forthright portrayal of the often bittersweet experience of being a teenager. They also find it simply interesting to read.

CHAPTER THREE

The Plot

T*he Outsiders* begins with its fourteen-year-old narrator, Ponyboy Curtis, stating, "When I stepped out into the bright sunlight from the darkness of the movie house, I had only two things on my mind: Paul Newman and a ride home."[20] He then proceeds to recount the thoughts that had crossed his mind as he walked home that day. Not least among those thoughts had been the ever-present danger for a greaser such as himself of getting jumped by their sworn enemies, the affluent Socs (pronounced "soshes").

As Ponyboy had feared, he is trailed by a red Corvair filled with Socs. He is indeed jumped; the Socs hold a switchblade on him and proceed to beat him. Luckily, he is rescued by the chance arrival of his brothers, Darry and Sodapop, and other members of their gang, including Dallas Winston, who is the only truly hardened criminal among them, and Two-Bit Mathews, who is frequently drunk and who always carries a switchblade. Ponyboy is shaken and has a few minor bruises and cuts, but he is otherwise fine.

The following night Ponyboy accompanies several of his fellow greasers—including his sixteen-year-old best friend Johnny—to the drive-in. Though admission to the drive-in is only a quarter, they choose to sneak in by climbing over the back fence. They meet two girls, Cherry Valance and her friend Marcia, both of whom are Socs. The girls had gone to the drive-in with their boyfriends but left the car when the boys began to drink. Dallas proceeds to make rude remarks to the girls, whereupon Cherry throws her soda in his face.

The ordinarily mild-mannered Johnny rebuffs the volatile Dallas in an effort to protect Cherry. "If it had been me," notes Ponyboy, "or Two-Bit, or Soda or Steve, or anyone but Johnny, Dally would have flattened him without a moment's hesitation. You just didn't tell Dally Winston what to do."[21] However, Dallas, as with all the other members of the gang, has a soft spot in his heart for Johnny due to the severe abuse and neglect Johnny suffers at home, and he leaves in a huff.

In a scene from the film, Ponyboy tells Cherry that Johnny was beaten up by a group of Socs. Cherry tries to convince him that not all Socs are this cruel.

Ponyboy and Cherry begin to talk, and Ponyboy tells her of the time when Johnny was jumped by a group of Socs and nearly beaten to death. He tells her of how the beating had left Johnny traumatized, and that Johnny now carries a six-inch switchblade that he intends to use if he ever finds himself in the same situation. Cherry is upset by the story and urges Ponyboy to believe that not all Socs are so cruel.

The Fatal Encounter

After the movie Ponyboy, Johnny, and Two-Bit agree to give the girls a ride home. As they walk toward Two-Bit's house to get his car, they encounter a blue Mustang filled with Socs, including Cherry's boyfriend, Bob Sheldon. Cherry and Marcia finally agree to get in the car in order to prevent the

Cherry's boyfriend Bob Sheldon (left), one of five drunken Socs who attack Ponyboy and Johnny at the park.

boys from fighting. Before getting in the car, Cherry informs Ponyboy that she thinks she could fall in love with Dallas Winston and that she fears she will if she ever sees him again. Meanwhile, Johnny recognizes Bob Sheldon as being one of the Socs who had nearly beaten him to death but says nothing.

Ponyboy and Johnny lie down in the vacant lot near Ponyboy's house in order to gaze at the stars and talk. Ponyboy speaks of his parents' fatal car accident that had occurred earlier that year, and Johnny talks about his abusive parents. They both agree that they would like to live "someplace without greasers or Socs, with just people. Plain ordinary people."[22]

Ponyboy and Johnny fall asleep in the vacant lot and wake up several hours later. Ponyboy hurries home to find his protective oldest brother, Darry, waiting up for him. Ponyboy interprets Darry's harsh treatment of him as an indication of Darry's growing dislike for him, and the two engage in a heated argument in which Darry hits Ponyboy for the first time. Darry is stunned by his own actions and doesn't stop Ponyboy from running out of the house. Ponyboy finds Johnny and recounts what happened. "I think I like it better when the old man's hitting me," Johnny says of his own father's physical abuse. "At least then I know he knows who I am. I walk in that house, and nobody notices."[23]

When Ponyboy and Johnny go to the park to discuss their plans of running away, they encounter the blue Mustang again. They are jumped by five drunken Socs, including Cherry's boyfriend, Bob Sheldon. Bob and several other Socs dunk Ponyboy's head beneath the water of a fountain for a prolonged period of time. Ponyboy begins to drown, but before he loses consciousness completely, his assailants release him. After catching his breath, Ponyboy realizes that Johnny has fatally stabbed Bob and that the other boys have fled. Ponyboy and Johnny do the same, leaving Bob to die.

From Hoodlums to Heroes

Scared and confused, Ponyboy and Johnny consult Dallas, who gives them some money and a gun and instructs them to hide out in an abandoned church that he knows of out in the country. The boys go to the church, where they live on bologna sandwiches, smoke cigarettes, and read *Gone with the Wind* and the Robert Frost poem "Nothing Gold Can Stay" to each other. Dallas comes to see them after five days and takes them to a restaurant in a nearby town, where Johnny announces that he wants to return home and turn himself into the police.

On their way home, they see that the church is engulfed in flames, and they suspect that the fire started as a result of one of their smoldering cigarettes. Ponyboy and Johnny suddenly notice that a few small children who must have been explor-

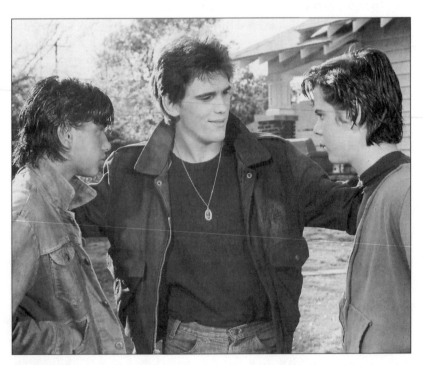

After Johnny (left) fatally stabs Bob, he and Ponyboy, feeling frightened and bewildered, turn to Dallas (center) for advice.

ing the abandoned building are now trapped inside. Heedless of the danger, Ponyboy and Johnny rush in to save them. They manage to rescue the children, but a piece of heavy burning timber falls on Johnny and critically injures him as he pushes Ponyboy from the building. Dallas also badly burns his arm as he drags Johnny from the fire.

Johnny and Dallas are hospitalized, and Ponyboy meets his brothers in the hospital waiting room. When Ponyboy sees that Darry is moved to tears by the sight of him uninjured, he realizes that he had been wrong about Darry and makes up with him. Ponyboy visits Johnny and gives him another copy of *Gone with the Wind*. He then visits Dallas, who expresses dismay about not being able to participate in the big rumble that is scheduled for that evening between the Socs and the greasers. The two gangs had agreed that no weapons were to be used in the rumble and, further, that the losers of the rumble must stay on their own side of town from now on.

The rumble occurs, with Dallas having left his hospital bed to attend. Ponyboy also participates despite a fever he has developed and suffers a concussion during the fight. The Socs flee, and the greasers win the rumble. Dallas and Ponyboy rush to the hospital to tell Johnny of their victory, where they find him dying. He tells them that violence is pointless and tells Ponyboy to "stay gold," in reference to the Robert Frost poem that they had read together.

Tragedy Strikes

Johnny dies, and his death is more than Dallas can bear. Dallas rushes from the hospital and impulsively robs a grocery store with an unloaded gun, knowing that the police will catch him. Ponyboy and his brothers arrive at the vacant lot near their house, where the police have surrounded Dallas. When Dallas points the unloaded gun at the police, they shoot him dead. Ponyboy, who is still reeling from his concussion, collapses at the sight of Dallas being shot.

Johnny's tragic death pushes Dallas to a point of desperation, and he impulsively robs a grocery store with an unloaded gun.

After remaining unconscious for several days, Ponyboy awakens at home in a confused state. He is in denial about Johnny's death and has convinced himself that it was he, rather than Johnny, who killed Bob Sheldon. Consequently, he decides to confess to the crime at the upcoming court hearing for Bob's murder.

At the hearing, however, the other Socs who had been present when Bob died admit that Johnny had killed Bob in order to save Ponyboy's life. Thus, Ponyboy's intentions of confessing have been thwarted. Despite his resulting acquittal and his acceptance of the fact that it was Johnny who killed Bob, Ponyboy is still despondent over Johnny's death and finds that he has grown emotionally numb. Though he feels some sympathy for his brother Sodapop, whose girlfriend has left him, Ponyboy is unable to shake his overwhelming sense of emotional detachment.

Staying Gold

Ponyboy's emotional numbness finally subsides when he discovers a note to him from Johnny in their copy of *Gone with the Wind*. In the note Johnny explains that he now understands the Robert Frost poem they had read, stating, "He meant

Dallas's self-destructiveness results in tragedy. Here, he lies dead, having been shot by the police after pointing his unloaded gun at them.

you're gold when you're a kid. . . . Like the way you dig sunsets, Pony. That's gold. Keep that way, it's a good way to be."[24] The note revives Ponyboy emotionally and inspires him to work on an essay that had been assigned at school. He phones the teacher who had assigned the essay and asks if there is a limit to the number of pages that the essay can have. When the teacher tells him that there is not, Ponyboy proceeds to write the essay in an effort to help the many other underprivileged, nearly hopeless greasers who "ached for something better," and in the hopes that, by telling the greasers' side of the story, "people would understand . . . and wouldn't be so quick to judge a boy by the amount of hair oil he wore."[25]

Ponyboy begins the essay (and ends the novel) with the same distinctive sentence with which he had begun his narration of the novel: "When I stepped out into the bright sunlight from the darkness of the movie house, I had only two things on my mind: Paul Newman and a ride home."[26]

CHAPTER FOUR

The Cast of Characters

T he characters in *The Outsiders* belong to one of two rival gangs: the affluent Socs from the west side of town or the underprivileged greasers from the east side of town.

Johnny Cade

Johnny, one of the story's main characters, is a quiet, shy sixteen-year-old greaser. Johnny, like his best friend, Ponyboy, feels a combination of pride and shame at being a greaser. He depends on the support of his greaser friends, yet he is also acutely aware that greasers are looked upon as nothing more than hoodlums.

Johnny is physically and emotionally abused by his parents, and while he does take comfort from the support of his fellow gang members, he explains to Ponyboy, "It ain't the same as having your own family care about you. . . . It just ain't the same."[27] Johnny is also still traumatized and physically scarred by a severe beating that he received at the hands of the Socs. For these reasons, Johnny holds a special place in the gang—even the hardened Dallas has a soft spot for him. Johnny seems to represent for them the innocence they have lost, and they all seek to protect him from harm.

While Johnny is impressed by the gallantry of the southern gentlemen in *Gone with the Wind*, he isn't able to see that his painful life has afforded him with his own sense of nobility. This becomes increasingly evident in the story as he begins to take his stand: by standing up to Dallas on Cherry's behalf; by

Greasers Dallas, Ponyboy, and Johnny (from left to right) are close friends from the wrong side of the tracks.

saving Ponyboy from the Socs; by comforting Ponyboy as they hide out; by saving the children and Ponyboy from the burning church; and, finally, by his last-ditch deathbed effort to preserve Ponyboy's idealism. Indeed, as his note serves to revive Ponyboy emotionally and seems to inspire him to leave behind the violent gang life, Johnny emerges as the true hero of the story.

Darrel "Darry" Curtis

Darry is the legal guardian of Ponyboy and Sodapop and is also the leader of their small gang of greasers. He is twenty years old, six feet two, broad shouldered, muscular, and handsome. He became the guardian of his two younger brothers when their parents died in a car accident eight months previous to the story's outset. Prior to that he had been a star high school football player who had won athletic scholarships to college, but since his parents' deaths he has had to work two jobs in order to keep the family together. Ponyboy describes him as "getting old before his time trying to run a family and hold on to two jobs and never having any fun."[28]

Darry fears that his brothers will be sent to foster homes if they get in trouble, and this fear causes him to be relatively strict with them. He has assumed the role of father, a role with which he is not entirely comfortable. Because of Ponyboy's exceptional intelligence, he holds him to particularly high academic standards. He has sacrificed his own dreams and is instead investing his energy in Ponyboy's future.

Darry's expectations of Ponyboy cause significant conflict between them. Ponyboy's inability to comprehend Darry's motives is evident when he states:

> If I brought home B's, he wanted A's, and if I got A's, he wanted to make sure they stayed A's. If I was playing football, I should be in studying, and if I was reading, I should be out playing football. He never hollered at

Sodapop—not even when Soda dropped out of school or got tickets for speeding. He just hollered at me.[29]

On some issues, however, Darry is particularly lenient with the boys. In addition to letting them smoke cigarettes, for example, he eats chocolate cake with them every morning for breakfast and frequently roughhouses with them.

Though Darry's role in the story is relatively minor, he does provides a source of authority for Ponyboy to rebel against. This serves to further the sense of isolation that Ponyboy already feels as a greaser, an orphan, and as someone whose best friend has died, and helps to facilitate the eventual resolution of this sense of isolation as he gains a deeper understanding of Darry's love.

Ponyboy Curtis

Ponyboy is the story's narrator and one of its main characters. Compared to other characters such as Dallas or Johnny, Ponyboy's altruistic character is, for the most part, revealed from the outset of the story. Thus, his reliability as narrator is strong; he offers little cause for doubt that the way he is telling the story is accurate.

At age fourteen, Ponyboy is already well acquainted with life's tragedies and the dark side of human nature. Intelligent, sensitive, and idealistic, Ponyboy struggles to preserve these qualities—to "stay gold," as the Robert Frost poem says—while confronting a staggering and demoralizing array of difficulties.

Orphaned eight months earlier when a car crash took their parents' lives, Ponyboy and his oldest brother, Darry, who is now Ponyboy's legal guardian, struggle to redefine their relationship with each other. As might be expected of any normal fourteen-year-old, Ponyboy resists the authority that Darry attempts to impose on him and is oblivious to the pressure that Darry now faces as his guardian. As Ponyboy grapples

The faces of Ponyboy (left), Steve (center), and Two-Bit reveal the tension caused by the greasers' conflict with the Socs.

with the series of misfortunes that befall him, however, the love behind Darry's anger and heavy-handedness becomes evident to him.

Ponyboy feels conflict over his identity as a greaser. He is torn between the love and loyalty he feels toward his fellow greasers and his desire to be seen as something more than just a low-class hoodlum. Further, as the story unfolds, he is increasingly disillusioned by the senseless, relentless violence that has been so central to his experience as a greaser. However, he finds himself aspiring to the older Dallas Winston's hardened, insensitive approach to life when he is faced with Johnny's and Dallas's deaths. After finding a note from Johnny urging him to protect and value his fragile ideal-istic outlook, Ponyboy begins to embrace his repressed feel-ings of sorrow and confusion.

At the story's end, as Ponyboy begins to write his life story, it becomes clear that through the introspective power of writ-ing, he will become something more than just a greaser—that he will find himself. As he writes about having "stepped out into the bright sunlight from the darkness of the movie house,"[30] it seems that he is also stepping out into the prover-bial light, and thus, that he will indeed stay gold.

Sodapop Curtis

Sodapop is Ponyboy's second-oldest brother and is the person that Ponyboy most loves and idolizes. He is easygoing and wears a perpetual, contagious grin. He is handsome, with blond hair and "lively, dancing, recklessly laughing eyes that can be sympathetic one moment and blazing with anger the next."[31]

Soda found school difficult and believes himself to be unintelligent. Consequently, he was happy to drop out of high school at age sixteen to work at a gas station, believing that his time would be better spent helping to support the household. He also rides in rodeos and loves horses, and Ponyboy recalls how, while working part-time at a stable, Sodapop once grew very attached to a particular horse that was kept there and was deeply saddened when the horse was moved to another stable.

When Darry and Ponyboy quarrel, it is Sodapop who plays peacemaker. He tries to keep Darry off Ponyboy's back and tries to make Ponyboy understand that Darry is acting out of love for him. Sodapop has a girlfriend named Sandy whom he loves and wants to marry, yet in the end Sandy leaves him, and the sadness that Sodapop feels over Johnny's and Dallas's deaths is thus compounded.

Overall, though, Sodapop is a relatively minor charac-ter whose purpose in the story seems primarily to be to periodically remind the reader of the motives behind Darry's strictness.

Keith "Two-Bit" Mathews

Two-Bit is six feet tall, stocky, with long rusty-colored side-burns and gray eyes. He got his nickname because he never stops making wisecracks and always has to get his two bits in. He is notorious among greasers for his heavy drinking, his habitual shoplifting, and for the black-handled switchblade he carries. At age eighteen and a half, he is still a junior in high school. As with the rest of the gang, he is protective of Johnny and doesn't allow anyone—not even Ponyboy—to give him a hard time. He is a minor character in the story, and his primary function in the plot is to provide comic relief.

Steve Randall

Steve, a tall, lean seventeen-year-old, has been Sodapop's best friend since grade school. Cocky and smart, Steve works as a part-time mechanic at the same gas station as Sodapop. His knowledge of cars also makes him adept at stealing parts off them. Steve doesn't like Ponyboy and considers him a tagalong because Sodapop always brings him whenever they go anywhere. Steve's character serves only a minor role in the story.

Bob Sheldon

Bob is Cherry Valance's handsome Soc boyfriend. Seemingly altogether devoid of a conscience, Bob serves as the story's primary antagonist. He wears heavy rings on his fingers, and it was these rings that left Johnny's face permanently scarred after Bob and a number of other Socs jumped Johnny and nearly beat him to death before the novel begins. Bob's death serves to complicate the plot and to begin Ponyboy and Johnny's earnest reevaluation of their own identities and the tragic lives they lead.

Sherri "Cherry" Valance

Nicknamed for her red hair, Cherry is a rich, beautiful Soc. Intelligent, sensitive, and fond of gazing at sunsets, she is not altogether unlike Ponyboy. She is surprised to find that she likes Ponyboy and Johnny and that she feels a strong attraction to Dallas despite his crudeness. She is saddened when she hears the story of Johnny's having been beaten by Socs and feels sympathy for the rough breaks that Ponyboy and the other greasers must endure. However, she also feels unable to venture outside the comfort of her Soc peer group and fears what her parents would do if they saw her with greasers.

Cherry is a minor character in the story who serves to humanize the Socs for Ponyboy. She shows him that not all Socs are cruel and that, despite their affluence, they, too, must suffer in life.

Dallas "Dally" Winston

Dallas is perhaps the most compelling character in the story. He is the only truly hardened criminal in the gang and is described by Ponyboy as "dangerous and tougher than the rest of us—tougher, colder, meaner," and as having eyes of "blue, blazing ice, cold with a hatred of the whole word."[32] Dallas has been in and out of jail since the age of ten and participated in bloody, organized gang wars on the West Side of New York City. Though it is not stated when or why Dally left New York City, it is clear that he is fiercely loyal to this small gang of greasers in which he now finds himself.

In addition to being the toughest, Dallas is also the most emotionally complex character in the story. The only evidence of his humanity lies in his tender feelings for Johnny and his reverence of Johnny's innocence and fragility. As Ponyboy notes, "Johnny was the only thing Dally loved."[33] Notwithstanding his love for Johnny, Dallas's toughness borders on the suicidal, and he seems—on the surface—to be otherwise impervious to emotions.

Dallas is the most complex and charismatic character in the story. He is played in the film by Matt Dillon, seen here in conversation on the set with director Francis Ford Coppola.

Dallas tries to convince Ponyboy to be more like him, telling him, "You'd better wise up, Pony. . . . [Y]ou get tough like me and you don't get hurt. You look out for yourself and nothing can touch you."[34] Of course, the very fact that Dallas is concerning himself with Ponyboy's emotional well-being calls into question his ability to follow his own formula, as does his heroic act of rescuing Johnny from the church fire late in the novel. The extent of Dallas's emotional vulnerability is revealed in the end as he loses his will to live when Johnny dies.

The presence of Dallas Winston in the story serves Ponyboy's growth as well. Dallas's supposed lack of feeling appeals to Ponyboy when he is faced with Johnny's and Dallas's deaths, and for a time Ponyboy aspires to this frame of mind. However, unlike Dallas, Ponyboy is able to realize before it's too late that his efforts to be insensitive are futile—that he is merely trying to hide from himself.

CHAPTER FIVE

Literary Criticism

The body of literary criticism that has been written in response to *The Outsiders* is considerably smaller than that of most other groundbreaking literary works. This is most likely due to the fact that, unlike most literary landmarks, *The Outsiders* was written by a sixteen-year-old and, thus, is not as thematically complex. The literary criticism that does exist about *The Outsiders* evaluates the novel almost exclusively in terms of how successfully it achieves the realism to which it aspires.

For example, in one of the novel's first-ever literary reviews, *Kirkus Reviews*—one of the publishing industry's most respected journals—states: "You can believe a teen-ager wrote it but you can bet teen-agers won't believe what it says."[35] This quote provides an excellent illustration of the fact that the analyses of literary critics don't necessarily reflect popular opinion—*The Outsiders'* appeal to young readers certainly attests to this fact.

This is also not to suggest, however, that literary analysis of the work is fruitless. On the contrary, by carefully considering the views of literary critics on *The Outsiders*—even those views that seem to oppose one's own feelings about it—a reader can further define the reasons why he or she feels a certain way about the novel, and thereby arrive at a deeper understanding, and perhaps appreciation, of it. Indeed, literary critics themselves often use the views of other critics on a particular literary work to help them identify their own views on that work. And, as with all literary breakthroughs, *The Outsiders* has received reviews that range from favorable to not so favorable, many of which offer thought-provoking examinations of numerous aspects of the story's realism.

Readers might, for example, arrive at a deeper understanding and appreciation of the various characters in the story by examining the critical viewpoints of others on the story's characterization. As with most authors, Hinton constructs the characters in *The Outsiders* through a variety of means, including descriptions and background information, as well as through the characters' actions in the story. Also, since Ponyboy Curtis is both a character in the story as well as the story's narrator, he provides additional insight into his character through direct accounts of his own thoughts and feelings. The extent to which these components come together in *The Outsiders* to form characters that ring true for a given reader largely determines the extent to which the reader cares about the outcome of the story.

The Reality of the Characters

Literary critics differ on the extent to which the teen characters in *The Outsiders* ring true. Literary critic A. Abigail McCormick, for example, does not find the novel's characters realistic. She suggests that "Hinton gives her characters enough flexibility to keep them from being complete stereotypes, but they are never wholly believable as real people." McCormick, however, also seems to feel that these characters' stereotypical tendencies work to the story's advantage, noting, "The story explores the divisions and similarities between people, and challenges the reader to question the apparently clear-cut categorizations of certain characters." She also concedes that "readers will identify with the confusion felt by the characters and with Ponyboy's struggles to be an individual while remaining one of the gang. Although the characters are stereo-types, they possess a truthful simplicity."[36]

The *London Times,* for its part, does not feel that there are any stereotypical aspects to Ponyboy's character that require forgiveness from the reader, as it declares, "Ponyboy is a cred-ible character. . . . Young readers will adopt [him] as a kind of folk hero for both his exploits and his dialogue."[37] John S. Simmons also praises wholeheartedly the manner in which Hinton renders Ponyboy in the novel, stating:

> Ponyboy's naiveté, lack of sophistication and commit-ment to an established lifestyle give the novel its tone. Amazingly, the author, a teenage female, has created a credible teenage male protagonist/narrator. In doing so, she has contributed significantly to the new realism of the contemporary young adult novel.[38]

John Rowe Townsend, however, suggests that the novel romanticizes and oversimplifies the experiences of underprivi-leged teens, commenting, "It may be noted that, just as slum children in novels by middle-class writers can easily be nice middle-class children under the skin, so the greasers in this book by 'a seventeen-year-old whose best friends are greasers' sometimes look like sheep in wolves' clothing."[39] Simmons, on the other hand, who considers at length Hinton's portrayal of underprivileged teens in *The Outsiders,* argues that the novel exposes readers to the real adversities faced by underprivileged teens:

> One of Susan Hinton's significant achievements in *The Outsiders* is to hold up for scrutiny young people from economically, culturally, and socially deprived circum-stances. In Ponyboy Curtis, his brothers Sodapop and Darry, and his "Greaser" companions, Hinton has introduced readers, most of whom have probably been

from white, middle class origins, to the desires, the priorities, the frustration, the preoccupations, and above all, the anger of those young people who may live in the seedier parts of town but who have established a code of behavior which reflects (to the dismay of some) their sense of dignity and self-worth.[40]

Lillian N. Gerhardt suggests that the novel's depiction of underprivileged teens is not only of benefit to middle-class readers, but also to underprivileged readers themselves:

Ponyboy, the 14-year-old narrator, tells how it looks and feels from the wrong side of the tracks. . . . The story is exciting and those difficult-to-serve kids at the culturally detached bottom of society can respond to this book, with its revelations of the latent decency of the urban slum characters, who are nearly but not yet hopeless.[41]

Ruth Cox, in a review written more than thirty years after the novel's first publication, suggests that the story's underprivileged teen characters continue to accurately depict the experiences and social realities faced by many modern-day teens, noting:

Ponyboy's hair was greased and long. Today it might be shaved or dyed. There still are 14-year-old "greasers" who do well in school and know about Robert Frost and Jack London. And yes, young adults like Dallas, who see no future for themselves, die in bursts of gunfire on our streets.[42]

Simmons finds that Darry Curtis's character in particular has come to reflect the experiences of a growing number of underclass teens who have also grown up too soon, writing:

Darry has taken on an adult role and, given his limited education and financial resources, does the best he can. It is through his character that readers perceive the fight for survival an underclass situation. But Darry, perhaps more than the other Greasers, accepts his lot stoically and with dignity. He asks for neither material aid nor sympathy. To provide what is needed for family survival, he works longer hours and enforces house rules. In Darry, Hinton has added a note of prophecy to her story. As have countless young single parents of America's 1990's, he has become an adult before his time.[43]

Indeed, though perhaps most true of Darry's character, becoming an adult before one's time is an experience that is shared by all of the story's greaser characters. So central, in fact, is this experience to the story, it could also be said to summarize the story's plot. And this stands to reason, since the plot of any story is largely created by the actions of the story's characters.

The Credibility of the Plot

Since plot is largely an extension of character, it is also not so surprising that many of those critics who perceive weaknesses within the characterization of *The Outsiders* also find weaknesses within its plot and that, likewise, those who give high praise to the story's characterization also praise its plot. This sort of consistency isn't always present within a given critical analysis of this novel, however. For example, while finding Ponyboy's character to be "credible," the *London Times* also says of the story that "the plot creaks and the ending is wholly factitious."[44]

Other critics also suggest that the plot of *The Outsiders* is lacking resolution in some way. In a review written shortly after the book was released in 1967, the *Saturday Review* expresses dissatisfaction with the story's ending, stating, "There is an easing of tension and a growth toward maturity by the close of the story, but no magical change, no pat finale."[45] In another review written at the time of the book's first publication, Thomas Fleming states, "The final confrontation between Ponyboy and the Socs, in which he realizes they too are pretty mixed-up kids, is a comforting if not quite believable ending."[46]

Depicting Class Struggle

Fleming also faults the way in which class struggle is depicted in *The Outsiders*, commenting:

> Apparently in Tulsa, where Miss Hinton sets her story, the poor guys don't beat up the rich guys. It works the other way around—and she uses this switch to build up quite a head of self-pitying steam for her hero and his friends. This, I must admit, runs somewhat counter to my own teenage experience; in my old home town, even *semi*-socs were the ones who got their lumps.[47]

> Respected critic and author Nat Hentoff suggests that there is, in fact, social value and universal appeal in Hinton's tale of rivalry between Socs and greasers, writing:

> Any teenager, no matter what some of his textbooks say, knows that this is decidedly not a classless society, and *The Outsiders* examines the social and physical warfare between a group of slum youngsters, "the greasers," and the progeny of the upper middle class in Tulsa, "the Socs." Miss Hinton, with an astute ear and a lively sense of the restless rhythms of the young, also explores the tenacious loyalties on both sides of the class divide.[48]

Townsend also finds the story's initial premise viable, stating, "Its background appears authentic." However, similar to the complaint he registers about overly romanticized characters, he also suggests that "true feeling is hopelessly entangled with false, bad-film sentimentality, and the plot is creakingly unbelievable."[49]

Sentimentality

Excessive sentimentality is, in fact, a relatively common criticism of the plot of *The Outsiders*. Gerhardt, for example, whose review was written shortly after the first publication of the novel, says, "Compassionate understanding sometimes crosses over into sentimentalization and the story could have used some strong comic relief." Gerhardt, who found out shortly after writing this review that Hinton is a female, attached to her review an addendum that notes: "In retrospect the obvious clue [that Hinton is a female] is that maybe only a girl could broadcast, without alibi, the soft centers of these boys and how often they do give way to tears."[50]

McCormick also criticizes the plot's sentimentality, arguing, "At times the plot . . . is a bit melodramatic, as in Dally's self-contrived death and Johnny's dying words, a reference to Robert Frost's poem 'Nothing Gold Can Stay.'" However, just as McCormick is willing to forgive the story's stereotyped characters, she is also willing to forgive in this matter: "While such sentimentality may detract from readers' enjoyment of the story, the book's intensity and essential truthfulness make up for any shortcomings in plot."[51]

A defense of the plot's sentimentality is offered by popular young-adult novelist Richard Peck, who states simply, *"The Outsiders* portrays the warmth of belonging to a group that all young people need. . . . [I]t tells an exciting tale in unabashedly melodramatic terms."[52] A similar defense of the story's sentimentality in the *English Journal* notes that shortly after the story's publication, while some adults were reluctant to believe that the teen-agers described or the events portrayed in the book were realistic . . . the story is a gripping one, told honestly and fearlessly with a good deal of psychological understanding. *The Outsiders* is guaranteed to be read with relish.[53]

Obviously, this prediction by the *English Journal* has proven more accurate than that of *Kirkus Reviews*, as *The Outsiders* continues to be "read with relish" more than thirty years after it was written by the sixteen-year-old Hinton. Perhaps it is precisely the honesty and fearlessness with which Hinton describes teenagers and portrays events—the very things that some adults find unrealistic about the story—that have made the story so enduring with teens. At any rate, there is clearly something in Hinton's story that continues to speak powerfully to them, and, in the final analysis, perhaps it is teens themselves who are best qualified to explain what that something is.

Notes

Introduction: Inside *The Outsiders*

1. S. E. Hinton, "S. E. Hinton," in *Speaking for Ourselves: Autobiographical Sketches by Notable Authors of Books for Young Adults.* Urbana, IL: National Council of Teachers of English, 1990, p. 95.

Chapter 1: The Life of S. E. Hinton

2. Quoted in Jay Daly, *Presenting S. E. Hinton*, 2nd ed. Boston: Twayne, 1989, p. 2.

3. Daly, *Presenting S. E. Hinton*, p. 2.

4. Quoted in Daly, *Presenting S. E. Hinton*, p. 2.

5. Random House website, Authors and Illustrators Index, www.randomhouse.com/teachers/authors/sehi.html.

6. John S. Simmons, "A Look Inside a Landmark: *The Outsiders*," in *Censored Books: Critical Viewpoints*, edited by Nicholas J. Karolides, Lee Burress, and John M. Kean. London: Scarecrow Press, 1993, p. 440.

7. Randomhouse website.

8. Quoted in David Smith, "Hinton, What Boys Are Made Of," *Los Angeles Times*, July 15, 1982.

9. Quoted in Daly, *Presenting S. E. Hinton*, p. 3.

10. Randomhouse website.

11. Randomhouse website.

12. Randomhouse website.

13. Randomhouse website.

Chapter 2: Redefining Young Adult Fiction

14. Quoted in Daly, *Presenting S. E. Hinton*, p. 2.

15. Daly, *Presenting S. E. Hinton*, p. 17.

16. Daly, *Presenting S. E. Hinton*, preface.

17. Quoted in Simmons, "A Look Inside a Landmark," p. 433.

18. Simmons, "A Look Inside a Landmark," p. 439.

19. S. E. Hinton, "Teenagers Are for Real," *New York Times Book Review*, August 27, 1967. Reprinted in *Children's Literature*

Review, vol. 3, edited by Gerald J. Senick. Detroit: Gale Research, 1978, p. 69.

Chapter 3: The Plot

20. S. E. Hinton, *The Outsiders.* 1967. Reprint, New York: Puffin Books, 1997, p. 1.
21. Hinton, *The Outsiders*, p. 24.
22. Hinton, *The Outsiders*, p. 48.
23. Hinton, *The Outsiders*, p. 51.
24. Hinton, *The Outsiders*, p. 178.
25. Hinton, *The Outsiders*, p. 179.
26. Hinton, *The Outsiders*, p. 180.

Chapter 4: The Cast of Characters

27. Hinton, *The Outsiders*, pp. 51–52.
28. Hinton, *The Outsiders*, p. 43.
29. Hinton, *The Outsiders*, p. 13.
30. Hinton, *The Outsiders*, p. 180.
31. Hinton, *The Outsiders*, p. 8.
32. Hinton, *The Outsiders*, p. 10.
33. Hinton, *The Outsiders*, p. 152.
34. Hinton, *The Outsiders*, p. 147.

Chapter 5: Literary Criticism

35. *Kirkus Reviews*, April 15, 1967, pp. 506–507.
36. A. Abigail McCormick, *"The Outsiders,"* in *Beacham's Guide to Literature for Young Adults*, vol. 2, edited by Kirk H. Beetz and Suzanne Niemeyer. Washington, DC: Beacham, 1990, pp. 1,009, 1,010, 1,011.
37. *London Times Literary Supplement*, "On the Hook," October 30, 1970, p. 1,258.
38. Simmons, "A Look Inside a Landmark," p. 436.
39. John Rowe Townsend, *"The Outsiders,"* in *Children's Literature Review*, vol. 3, edited by Gerald J. Senick. Detroit: Gale Research, 1978, p. 71.

40. Simmons, "A Look Inside a Landmark," p. 435.

41. Lillian N. Gerhardt, *"The Outsiders," School Library Journal,* May 1967. Reprinted in *Children's Literature Review,* edited by Senick, p. 71.

42. Ruth Cox, "Old and New Paperback Favorites," *Teacher Librarian,* January/February 1999.

43. Simmons, "A Look Inside a Landmark," p. 436.

44. "On the Hook," p. 1,258.

45. *"The Outsiders," Saturday Review,* May 13, 1967, p. 21.

46. Thomas Fleming, *"The Outsiders," New York Times Book Review,* May 7, 1967, p. 12.

47. Fleming, *"The Outsiders,"* p. 12.

48. Nat Hentoff, *"The Outsiders,"* in *Children's Literature Review,* edited by Senick, p. 71.

49. Townsend, *"The Outsiders,"* p. 295.

50. Gerhardt, *"The Outsiders,"* p. 65.

51. McCormick, *"The Outsiders,"* pp. 1,011, 1,010–11.

52. Richard Peck, "In the Country of Teenage Fiction," *American Libraries,* April 1973, p. 204.

53. "Book Marks," *English Journal,* February 1969, p. 295.

For Further Exploration

Below are some suggestions for essays and themes to write about *The Outsiders.*

1. Identify Hinton's underlying message in *The Outsiders.* Analyze how well you think Hinton conveys that message, and tell whether you agree with it and why. *See* Patty Campbell, "The Young Adult Perplex," *Wilson Library Bulletin*, September 1985, pp. 61–63.

2. Identify the two goals that Ponyboy says he hopes to accomplish by telling his story. Offer specific reasons for why you do or do not think his telling his story is likely to accomplish these goals within his society. *See* McCormick, *"The Outsiders,"* pp. 1,007–14.

3. Imagine that S. E. Hinton is a student at your school and that she wrote *The Outsiders* about the teenagers in your community. Using specific examples, explain how the novel would be different and how it would be the same. *See* Steven L. VanderStaay, "Doing Theory: Words About Words About *The Outsiders,"* *English Journal*, November 1992, pp. 57–62.

4. After reading several critical responses to *The Outsiders*, write your own critical response to some of those critics' analyses of the novel. Cite specific viewpoints expressed by these critics, and explain in detail why you do or do not agree with them. *See* "S. E. Hinton," *Children's Literature Review*, edited by Gerald J. Senick, pp. 69–72.

5. Learn more about Hinton's life experiences, and tell whether this knowledge makes you like *The Outsiders* less or more, and why. *See* Hinton, "S. E. Hinton," in *Speaking for Ourselves*, pp. 95–96; and Daly, *Presenting S. E. Hinton*, chap. 1.

6. Consider Hinton's choice of the inner city as the setting for *The Outsiders*. Using specifics, explain how this setting serves to shape the personalities of the novel's various greaser characters. *See* McCormick, *"The Outsiders,"* pp. 1,007–14.

7. Some people feel that teens should not read about the sort of violence and other "adult" subject matter featured in *The Outsiders* and that young adult literature should instead seek to shelter its readers from life's harsh realities. Citing examples from

The Outsiders, explain why you do or do not agree with this assessment of the novel in particular and of young adult literature in general. *See* Simmons, "A Look Inside a Landmark: *The Outsiders*," pp. 431–41.

8. Based on your understanding of what it feels like to be accepted by some groups and rejected by others or of what it feels like to lose someone you love, analyze some of the actions taken by Ponyboy, and explain why these actions do or do not seem realistic to you. *See* VanderStaay, "Words About Words About *The Outsiders*," pp. 57–62.

9. Maintain a reading journal while reading *The Outsiders*, making a new entry in the journal for each chapter you complete. When you have finished reading the novel, use specific examples to explain how keeping this writing journal has affected your understanding of the novel. *See* Arthea J. S. Reed, *Reaching Adolescents: The Young Adult Book and the School*, p. 437.

10. Evaluate the ongoing animosity between greasers and Socs in *The Outsiders*. Offer possible explanations for why the conflict between them continues, and tell how it might be permanently resolved. *See* McCormick, "The Outsiders," pp. 1,007–14.

Appendix of Criticism

Challenging the Class Divide in America

The conflict between the poor and the upper classes is at the heart of this story. The Socs label everyone from the ghetto as hoods and in so doing deprive the greasers of their humanity. The greasers are also guilty of prejudging the Socs, although Hinton deemphasizes this point. Clearly, though, both sides are at fault: neither attempts to understand the other group's problems, and both act violently. The important point, which many critics overlook, is that Ponyboy offers a way out of this cycle of violence and retribution. . . . Ponyboy writes his story in order to spread a spirit of understanding among teens and adults who come from different backgrounds. The characters can all be divided along class lines and ultimately into "good guys" and "bad guys," but the story also explores the divisions and similarities between people, and challenges the reader to question the apparently clear-cut categorizations of certain characters. Ponyboy and Johnny are judged by their actions rather than by their appearances only when they save a group of children from the burning church building. Even though Johnny eventually dies from wounds sustained during the fire, *The Outsiders* is essentially a story of hope, for it suggests that divisions between characters are, in the end, surmountable.

A. Abigail McCormick, *"The Outsiders,"* in *Beacham's Guide to Literature for Young Adults*, vol. 2, edited by Kirk H. Beetz and Suzanne Niemeyer. Washington DC: Beacham, 1990, p. 1,011.

A Realistic Look at Class Hostilities

It is rare-to-unique among juvenile books (where even the nonfiction concentrates on positive aspects of American life and ignores its underside) to find a novel confronting the class hostilities which have intensified since the Depression. The setting of the story is a small Oklahoma city, which underscores the national scope of a current problem and by-passes the subliminal reactions that attach to major cities. The boys in this book are neither unimaginable urban sophisticates nor unassimilated Puerto Ricans or Negroes running berserk; they are the pioneer-stock legatees of Huckleberry Finn. Ponyboy, the 14-year-old narrator, tells how it looks and feels from the wrong side of the tracks and of guerrilla raids into his territory by the traditional, well-heeled enemy from the residential district, and the beating that led to a murder charge and two deaths. The story is exciting and those difficult-to-serve kids at the culturally detached bottom of society can respond to this book, with its revelations of the latent decency of the urban slum characters, who are nearly but not yet hopeless.

Lillian N. Gerhardt, *"The Outsiders," School Library Journal,*
May 1967. Reprinted in *Children's Literature Review,* vol. 3,
edited by Gerald J. Senick. Detroit: Gale Research, 1978, p. 71.

The Anger and Aspirations of Underprivileged Teens

One of Susan Hinton's significant achievements in *The Outsiders* is to hold up for scrutiny young people from economically, culturally, and socially deprived circumstances. In Ponyboy Curtis, his brothers Sodapop and Darry, and his "Greaser" companions, Hinton has introduced readers, most of whom have probably been from white, middle class origins, to the desires, the priorities, the frustrations, the preoccupations, and above all, the *anger* of those young people who may live in the seedier parts of town but who have established a code of behavior which reflects (to the dismay of some) their sense of dignity and self-worth. As developed by their author, there is little which has been considered contemptible, callous, or even objectionable about the Curtis brothers and most of their friends. Faced with poverty and limited opportunity, they maintain a certain determined optimism and aspiration for a better life. Most important, they believe in, trust, and support each other, all sentiments which can be universally admired despite the circumstances in which they are displayed.

John S. Simmons, "A Look Inside a Landmark: *The Outsiders,"*
in *Censored Books: Critical Viewpoints,* edited by Nicholas J.

Karolides, Lee Burress, and John M. Kean. London:
Scarecrow Press, 1993, p. 435.

Hinton's Transcendent Characters

Clearly there is more to this book than the novelty of its publication in those pre-Hinton, Mary-Jane-Goes-to-the-Prom years.
In fact there is something in *The Outsiders*, as there is in other
Hinton books, that transcends the restrictions of time and place,
that speaks to the reader directly. It has nothing to do with the
age of the author, and little to do with the so-called "realism" of
the setting. It does, however, have very much to do with the
characters she creates, their humanity, and it has everything to
do with her honesty. . . . Francis Ford Coppola, who filmed and
cowrote, with Hinton, the screen versions of *The Outsiders* and
Rumble Fish, called her "a real American novelist," straight out
of the tradition that runs from Herman Melville right up
through J. D. Salinger, and beyond. The myth of the American
hero, of the outlaw-individualist, of the "gallant," lives on in the
eyes of Ponyboy Curtis and Johnny Cade.

Jay Daly, *Presenting S. E. Hinton*, 2nd ed. Boston:
Twayne, 1989, preface.

Avoiding the Pitfalls of Young Adult Fiction

It seems to me that trying to write a valid novel for a young reader—
let's say a thirteen-year-old who is at a sensitive and troubled point in
life—is at least as important and far more challenging than writing a
"real, adult novel."

It's a harder job because of the pitfalls. No one who has passed
through adolescence can re-enter it with vision unblurred by per-
sonal nostalgia and the kind of publicity the current youth scene
receives. It's a great temptation to preach, to patronize, to pander,
to placate, and especially to propagandize. And, of course, most
writers of juvenile fiction will never see . . . let us say, twenty-five
again.

An exception to be mentioned at once is S. E. Hinton, whose
best-selling *The Outsiders* (Viking) was written when she was a
teen-ager. It is a novel full of unheeded hints for elder writers of

young fiction. *The Outsiders* portrays the warmth of belonging to a group that all young people need. Instead of the hard-edged realism of contemporary causes and faddish problems, it tells an exciting tale in unabashedly melodramatic terms. The world of newspapers and parents and school and foreign wars lies beyond the perimeters of a story about belonging.

Richard Peck, "In the Country of Teenage Fiction," *American Libraries*, April 1973, p. 204.

Sexism in *The Outsiders*

Perhaps the most curious problem with *The Outsiders* is its sexism. Hinton chooses to focus almost exclusively on male characters and has little to say, let alone anything positive, about the greasers' female counterparts. When Dally harasses Cherry and Marcia at the drive-in, Ponyboy says he would probably have joined in if the girls had been "our kind," but refrained because these were "nice" girls. For someone who crusades against labeling and stereotyping, Ponyboy exhibits an attitude that does not make sense.

A. Abigail McCormick, *"The Outsiders,"* in *Beacham's Guide to Literature for Young Adults*, vol. 2, edited by Kirk H. Beetz and Suzanne Niemeyer. Washington DC: Beacham, 1990, p. 1,012.

The Proper Measure of Violence

The action of the story continues nearly nonstop, pausing occasionally to look at the stars, or to talk about southern gentlemen, but only for a short time before rushing ahead. Much of the action is violent, often described vividly, sometimes melodramatically. "Someone put his hand over my mouth, and I bit it as hard as I could, tasting the blood running through my teeth." You don't get much more vivid than that.

For the most part, though, the violence fits. Hinton appears to have known instinctively how to balance introspection with action in just the proper measure to keep the reader hooked. . . . She wants things to *happen,* and happen they do, but there remains an inevitability to the story that saves it from being merely a recounting of a succession of fist fights.

Jay Daly, *Presenting S. E. Hinton*, 2nd ed.
Boston: Twayne, 1989, pp. 17–18.

An Omnipresent Concern for Survival

The theme of human fragility is given eloquent voice in *The Outsiders*. Violent confrontations with their rivals place the well-being of both gangs in constant jeopardy. The absence and indifference of parents leads most of the Greasers to the conclusion that they must pretty well fend for themselves. Death and serious, sometimes disabling, injury are possibilities which the latter group faces as a matter of course. . . . In an environment where the concern with survival is omnipresent, the joy and promise of youth are both perceived with irony by Ponyboy and his Greaser cohorts, a far cry from the idyllic teenage days described in so many novels written in the decades before Susan Hinton's first literary effort.

John S. Simmons, "A Look Inside a Landmark: *The
Outsiders*," in *Censored Books: Critical Viewpoints*, edited by
Nicholas J. Karolides, Lee Burress, and John M. Kean.
London: Scarecrow Press, 1993, p. 437.

Hinton's Use of Symbolism

The Outsiders contains a complex symbolic structure within a straightforward plot. Hinton uses symbolism to express class and character differences. For the greasers, long hair represents dignity and independence. . . . The greasers' hair also symbolizes the group's lower social status: the word "greaser" refers to the way the young men fix their hair. It is a derogatory term, although greasers have adopted it themselves.

On a broader symbolic scale, Hinton weaves archetypal images and situations into her story. Ponyboy and Johnny, for example, do not simply hide out in the country; they undergo a metamorphosis. Hinton carefully constructs their rites of passage to include the typical stages of this process. First, the boys are exiled: they must hide in the country, away from family and friends. . . . They cut their hair, thus breaking a major connection with their past lives and making themselves more open to change.

Their transition comes as a test, literally a trial by fire: the boys must decide in a few seconds whether or not to risk their own lives in an attempt to save the children in the burning church. They decide on the noblest course of action, and Johnny sustains an injury that proves fatal. Nevertheless, both boys are reborn in a sense: they come through the fire; they rescue their innocence and goodness, as symbolized by the children they save from the church; and they are proclaimed heroes.

A. Abigail McCormick, *"The Outsiders,"*
in *Beacham's Guide to Literature for Young Adults,*
vol. 2, edited by Kirk H. Beetz and Suzanne Niemeyer.
Washington, DC: Beacham, 1990, p. 1,010.

Chronology

1948
Susan Eloise Hinton born on July 22 in Tulsa, Oklahoma.

1963
Enters Will Rogers High School in Tulsa.

1964
Begins junior year at Will Rogers High School in Tulsa. Receives a D in creative writing class. Father diagnosed with brain cancer and becomes very ill. Begins writing *The Outsiders*.

1965
Father dies from brain cancer. Completes *The Outsiders*.

1966
Enrolls at University of Tulsa, majors in journalism.

1967
The Outsiders is published in April, is chosen as an honor book at the *Chicago Tribune*'s Children's Spring Book Festival, and is featured on the *New York Herald Tribune*'s Best Teenage Books list. Writes essay "Teenagers Are for Real," which is published in the *New York Times Book Review* in August.

1968
Writes "Rumble Fish" as a short story and publishes it.

1970
Graduates from University of Tulsa with a B. A. in education. Writes *That Was Then, This Is Now* during spring and summer. Marries David Inhofe in September.

1971
That Was Then, This Is Now published, chosen as an honor book at the *Chicago Tribune*'s Children's Spring Book Festival.

1975
Rumble Fish published as novel, is chosen by American Library Association as one of the best books of the year. *The Outsiders* receives *Media and Methods*' Maxi Award.

1979
Tex published. *The Outsiders* receives Massachusetts Children's Book Award.

1982
Tex film adaptation released in September, starring Matt Dillon. Hinton has small acting role in the film.

1983
The Outsiders film adaptation released in March, grossing $5 million during first weekend of release. Hinton has small acting role in film and cowrites the screenplay with director Francis Ford Coppola. Gives birth to son, Nicholas David, in August. *Rumble Fish* film adaptation released in October.

1985
That Was Then, This Is Now film adaptation released in November. *The Outsiders* adapted into a television series by Fox Television.

1988
Taming the Star Runner published. Hinton receives American Library Association/*School Library Journal*'s first annual Margaret A. Edwards Award.

1994
Big David, Little David published.

1995
The Puppy Sister published.

Works Consulted

Major Editions of *The Outsiders*

S. E. Hinton, *The Outsiders*. New York: Viking, 1967.

———, *The Outsiders*. Boston: G. K. Hall, 1989. Published in large print for young readers.

———, *The Outsiders*. New York: Puffin, 1997. Features new cover art intended to appeal to a new generation of readers.

Other Novels by Hinton

S. E. Hinton, *Rumble Fish*. New York: Delacorte Press, 1975. Based on Hinton's short story of the same name, in which a junior high school boy idolizes his older brother, the coolest, toughest guy in the neighborhood, and wants to be just like him.

———, *Taming the Star Runner*. New York: Delacorte Press, 1988. Sent to live with his uncle after a violent confrontation with his stepfather, sixteen-year-old Travis, an aspiring writer, finds life in a small Oklahoma town confining until he meets an eighteen-year-old horse trainer named Casey.

———, *Tex*. New York: Delacorte Press, 1979. The love between two teenage brothers helps to alleviate the harshness of their usually parentless life as they struggle to grow up.

———, *That Was Then, This Is Now*. New York: Viking Press, 1971. Sixteen-year-old Mark and Bryon have been like brothers since childhood, but now, as their involvement with girls, gangs, and drugs increases, their relationship seems to gradually disintegrate.

Children's Books by Hinton

S. E. Hinton, *Big David, Little David*. Illustrated by Alan Daniel. New York: Doubleday, 1995. When Nick learns that a kindergarten classmate and his own father not only look alike but have the same name, he wonders if they could possibly be the same person.

———, *The Puppy Sister*. Illustrated by Jacqueline Rogers. New York: Delacorte Press, 1995. A young boy is astonished when his new puppy begins to change into a human girl.

Other Publications by Hinton

S. E. Hinton, "Rumble Fish [short story]," *Nimrod*, a special literary supplement to the *University of Tulsa Alumni Magazine*, October 1968, p. 4. Hinton's inspiration for this story was a photo that she saw in a magazine of a young man on a motorcycle.

————, in *Speaking for Ourselves: Autobiographical Sketches by Notable Authors of Books for Young Adults.* Urbana, IL: National Council of Teachers of English, 1990, pp. 95–96. Hinton comments briefly on her life, her career in general, and *The Outsiders* in specific. Book features eighty-seven such autobiographical statements by authors of young adult fiction.

————, "Teenagers Are for Real," *New York Times Book Review*, August 27, 1967, pp. 26–29. This essay, published four months after the first publication of *The Outsiders*, argues that teenagers crave, and are entitled to, realistic fiction.

Interviews and Speeches

Patty Campbell, "The Young Adult Perplex," *Wilson Library Bulletin*. September 1985, pp. 61–63. Features a brief interview of Hinton, in which she discusses the main themes of *The Outsiders* and her reputation as the "Queen of the Young Adult Novel."

S. E. Hinton. Acceptance speech for YASD/SLJ Author Achievement Award, New Orleans, July 9, 1988. Audio recording.

Biographical Information

Laurie Collier and Joyce Nakamura, eds., "S. E. Hinton," *Major Authors and Illustrators for Children and Young Adults*, vol. 3. Detroit: Gale Research, 1993, pp. 1,117–20. Has a brief chapter on Hinton's life and career, and is interspersed with quotes from both Hinton and literary critics.

Jay Daly, *Presenting S. E. Hinton*, 2nd ed. Boston: Twayne, 1989. Features a biographical chapter that discusses Hinton's childhood in Tulsa and the various myths that have surfaced about her over the years. Also features a separate chapter on each of Hinton's young adult novels, including *The Outsiders*.

Randon House website, Authors and Illustrators Index, www. randomhouse.com/teachers/authors/sehi.html. Features

biographical information about Hinton and a brief interview with her.

David Smith, "Hinton, What Boys Are Made Of," *Los Angeles Times*,
July 15, 1982.

Literary Reviews and Criticism

Monique Brown, *"The Outsiders* Is Still in at 30," *School Library
Journal*, October 1997. Offers brief overview of the book's
history and mentions Puffin Books' thirtieth-anniversary
paperback edition, which features new cover art that is intended to appeal to a new generation of young adult readers.

Anne Commire, ed., "S. E. Hinton," *Something About the Author*,
vol. 19. Detroit: Gale Research, 1980. Contains critical analysis of Hinton's work and some biographical information.

Ruth Cox, "Old and New Paperback Favorites," *Teacher Librarian*,
January/February 1999, pp. 44–46. Briefly discusses the
enduring themes addressed in *The Outsiders* and notes that
the book continues to receive high praise from today's teen
readers.

English Journal, February 1969, p. 295. Favorable review of *The
Outsiders* that dismisses the doubts of other critics concerning
the story's believability.

Stephen Farber, "Directors Join the S. E. Hinton Fan Club," *New
York Times*, March 20, 1983, pp. 2, 19. Discusses the growing
interest of directors such as Francis Ford Coppola in adapting
Hinton's novels into film.

Thomas Fleming, *"The Outsiders,"* New York Times Book Review,
May 7, 1967, p. 12. Suggests that the novel's plot and characterization are overly sentimental, but that these flaws are for-
givable in light of Hinton's young age, and that they are
outweighed by the novel's authentic-sounding dialogue and
engagingly brisk pace.

Lillian N. Gerhardt, *"The Outsiders,"* reprinted in *Children's
Literature Review*, vol. 3, edited by Gerald J. Senick. Detroit:
Gale Research, 1978, p. 71. A favorable review of *The Outsiders*
which praises the novel for its realistic treatment of underprivileged teens and the class divide in America.

Nat Hentoff, *"The Outsiders,"* in *Children's Literature Review*, vol. 3,
edited by Gerald J. Senick. Detroit: Gale Research, 1978, p. 71.

A largely favorable review which praises *The Outsiders* for revealing to teens the class divisions in society to a far greater extent than either pop music or television have done.

D. L. Kirkpatrick, ed., *Twentieth Century Children's Writers*. New York: St. Martin's, 1978. Provides analysis of the themes and characters in *The Outsiders* and several other works by Hinton.

Kirkus Reviews, April 15, 1967, pp. 506–7. An early, unfavorable review of *The Outsiders* which incorrectly surmises that teens will find the novel unconvincing, and that Cherry Valence—one of the novel's Soc (affluent, socialite teen) characters—is Hinton's alter-ego.

London Times Literary Supplement, October 30, 1970, p. 1,258. A mixed review of the literary merits of *The Outsiders;* features a brief and succinct discussion of various themes addressed in the novel.

A. Abigail McCormick, *"The Outsiders,"* in *Beacham's Guide to Literature for Young Adults*, vol. 2, edited by Kirk H. Beetz and Suzanne Niemeyer. Washington, DC: Beacham, 1990, pp. 1,007–14. Features analysis of various aspects of *The Outsiders*, including plot, characterization, and themes. Also has some biographical information.

Richard Peck, "In the Country of Teenage Fiction," *American Libraries*, April 1973, pp. 204–7. Peck briefly praises *The Outsiders* for its authentic portrayal of teen emotions as he discusses the difficulties for adults in writing young adult fiction.

Arthea J. S. Reed, *Reaching Adolescents: The Young Adult Book and the School*. New York: CBS College Press, 1985. Offers broad survey of popular young adult novels, including *The Outsiders*, and suggests methods for getting students to think critically about these novels.

Saturday Review, *"The Outsiders,"* May 13, 1967, p. 21. An early, largely favorable review of *The Outsiders*. Offers a brief summary of plot and praises Hinton's writing style and powers of observation.

Gerald J. Senick, ed., "S. E. Hinton," *Children's Literature Review*, vol. 3. Detroit: Gale Research, 1978, pp. 69–72. Excerpts from a wide range of reviews, criticism, and commentary on *The Outsiders*, *Rumble Fish*, and *That Was Then, This Is Now*. Also has brief commentary from Hinton.

John S. Simmons, "A Look Inside a Landmark: *The Outsiders*," in *Censored Books: Critical Viewpoints*, edited by Nicholas J. Karolides, Lee Burress, and John M. Kean. London: Scarecrow Press, 1993, pp. 431–41. Assesses the impact of the realism in *The Outsiders* on young adult fiction. Provides comprehensive historical overview of the evolution of the young adult novel and appraises the impact of other recent novels as well.

Jean C. Stine and Daniel B. Marowski, eds., *Contemporary Literary Criticism*, vol. 30. Detroit: Gale Research, 1984. Excerpts from criticism of Hinton's works, including *The Outsiders*.

John Rowe Townsend, *"The Outsiders,"* in *Children's Literature Review*, vol. 3, edited by Gerald J. Senick. Detroit: Gale Research, 1978, p. 7. A brief, mixed review of *The Outsiders*. Praises seventeen-year-old Hinton for the novel's authentic background, but also suggests that the novel is excessively sentimental.

Steven L. VanderStaay, "Doing Theory: Words About Words About *The Outsiders*," *English Journal*, November 1992, pp. 57–62. Uses M. H. Abrams's critical theory from *The Mirror and the Lamp: Romantic Theory and the Critical Tradition* to analyze *The Outsiders* and to suggest methods for getting students to think critically about the novel.

Index

Picture Credits

About the Author

Todd Howard has an M. A. degree in English from California State University Long Beach, and has taught English classes at both the elementary school and college levels.